The Gift of Righteousness

The Gift of Righteousness

*

Exploring Issues in Righteousness

Written by: Christopher C. Young

The Gift of Righteousness
Exploring Issues in Righteousness

Front & Back Cover Designs by Kingdom Builders Publishing
Images developed from Microsoft Clip Art & Media

Kingdom Builders Publishing
an imprint of Kingdom Builders International Ministries

To order extra copies of this book, please visit:

www.lulu.com/freshmanna

Unless otherwise indicated, all of the scripture quotations are taken from the *Authorized King James Version* **of the Bible. Scripture quotations marked with NIV are taken from the** *New International Version* **of the Bible. Scripture quotations marked with NASV are taken from the** *New American Standard Version* **of the Bible. Scripture quotations marked with Amplified are taken from the** *Amplified Bible***.**

Dual ISBN: 978-1-60141-096-2 &

ISBN: 978-1-41169-877-2

Printed in the United States of America

Contents

Introduction

What is righteousness? How can I know that I am right with God? These questions have been the subject of controversy since the Church's early existence. However, the Christian has to understand that righteousness is in who we are and not what we do. More importantly, the Christian has to realize that ultimately righteousness is a gift. In this book, we will discuss how God from the beginning of creation planned for man to be righteous.

God created man without the influence of sin; that is, righteous. God created Adam in His image, which includes His characteristics and righteousness. Thus, Adam was righteous. Then God took one of Adam's ribs and created Eve. The scriptures tell us that the woman is the glory of the man (her husband). So, whatever image the man is in, his wife will reflect it. Eve was righteous because of Adam and Adam was righteous because of God. Therefore, they were a righteous couple.

Without commandments and good works, Adam and Eve were righteous. Their righteousness was inherit in their physical being because God created them in righteousness.

God told them to be fruitful and multiply. Adam and Eve were to populate the earth by the command of God. God intended for all of mankind to be righteous. Even though Adam and Eve failed to maintain their righteousness, God's plan never changed concerning righteous sons and daughters. Righteousness is a gift that is given by God to us as believers, but we must work to maintain it.

What is the work that we must do to maintain our righteousness? The answer is simple, Follow Christ! We must walk in obedience to God. Obedience is the key to maintaining our righteousness in God through Christ. Once we have accepted Christ as our personal Lord and Savior, God imputes righteousness to us. However, we must demonstrate this righteousness by faith through good works. Ephesians 4:24 states that believers should put on the new man which, after God, is created in righteousness and true holiness. In doing so, His gift of righteousness will not be bestowed upon us in vain.

1
The Beginning of Righteousness

For years, scholars and Christians have debated about the righteousness of God, and whether or not are we walking in it. The topic concerning the righteousness of God is quite simple, but we have made it difficult to walk in it because of our differences in opinions.

Some believe that we obtain true righteousness through works, while others believe that it is by faith. In this section, we will discuss the origin of righteousness and the origin of self-righteousness.

> ***And God said, Let us make man in our image, after our likeness: and let them have dominion over the fish of the sea, and over the fowl of the air, and over the cattle, and over all the earth, and over every creeping thing that creepeth upon the earth. (Genesis 1: 26)***

The Origin of Righteousness

God is the source of all things. When He decided to create man, He used Himself as the model. God stated that man would be made in His likeness and image. The man that He would create would reflect His nature and personality. The scriptures declare that righteousness along with love and holiness make up the nature of God.

> ***But let him that glorieth glory in this, that he understandeth and knoweth me, that I am the Lord which exercise loving-kindness, judgment, and righteousness, in the earth: for in these things I delight, saith the Lord. (Jeremiah 9:23)***

In the above scripture, If God made man in His image and likeness, then, man's very nature would mirror God's. Since God is the source of righteousness, then the man created would reflect His righteousness. However, man's righteousness would find definition in the righteousness that comes from God.

God made Adam in His image and Adam was therefore righteous. When God created Adam, he was righteous without works. God created him in His righteousness. Adam's righteousness would be established as long as he followed God's command.

At that time, God's command was that man was not to eat of the tree of the knowledge of good and evil.

> ***And the Lord God commanded the man, saying, Of every tree of the garden thou mayest freely eat: But of the tree of the knowledge of good and evil, thou shalt not eat of it: for in the day that thou eatest thereof thou shalt surely die. (Genesis 2:16-17)***

If Adam followed God's command, it would establish the righteousness that he had received from God at creation. He had to remain obedient to God. Some ask, "Why did God give him a choice by placing the tree in the garden?" God set the boundaries for righteousness. As long as Adam did not eat of the tree, he walked in righteousness before the Lord.

The Origin of Self-Righteousness

God is the origin of righteousness. Man has the ability to produce righteousness. However, man's righteousness usually manifests as self-righteousness. Self-righteousness usually occurs when man makes an addition to the righteous standards set by God. It occurs when men choose their own way of thinking about what is right or wrong above God's.

It is interesting to find in the story of creation how Eve developed her own standard in adhering to God's command. The Pharisees operated in a similar manner (to be discussed later) and it put them in opposition to God.

Eve and the Serpent

From Genesis 2:17, God commanded man not to eat of the tree of knowledge. However, Eve went beyond God's command and operated in self-righteousness.

> ***And the woman said unto the serpent, We may eat of the fruit of the trees of the garden: But of the fruit of the tree which is in the midst of the garden, God hath said, Ye shall not eat of it, neither shall ye touch it, lest ye die. (Genesis 3:2-3)***

When the serpent asked about God's command, her reply added to what God had said. She said that we may eat of every tree of the garden except the tree in the mist of the garden God said, You shall not eat of it, ***neither shall ye touch it***, lest ye die."

God's command did not include neither shall ye touch it. She established her own righteousness when she said, "Neither shall ye touch it, lest ye die." Self-righteousness results in unnecessary condemnation. When individuals operate in self-righteousness, if they break their own law, they are guilty aside from breaking God's command. This is what happened to Eve.

She condemned her own self by touching the fruit that God told them not to eat. She said that God said if you touch it, you will die, but that was false. She condemned herself, before God could judge her. In order for her to eat the forbidden fruit, she first had to have touched it with her fingers. By her own law, she was condemned.

Self-righteousness will bring man into God's judgment. Matthew 12:37 says, (Jesus speaking)

> ***For by thy words thou shalt be justified, and by thy words, thou shalt be condemned.***

Self-righteousness causes man to teach the precepts of men as if they are the commandments of God. This is how she was condemned before God could judge her. She presented to the serpent a standard that God had not instituted. From this story, we discover that self-righteousness leads to deception, which leads to disobedience. Eve fell victim to this process and involved her husband.

> ***Wherefore, as by one man sin entered into the world, and death by sin; and so death passed upon all men, for that all have sinned. (Romans 5:12)***

His involvement resulted in sin coming into the world and the absence of righteousness. The scriptures declare that man did what was right in his own eyes. Therefore, the Lord destroyed man, except Noah and his family.

Because of His love for man, God chose Israel and instituted the Law of Righteousness (the Mosaic Law) in order for man to understand His righteousness. In addition, He wanted man to be able to recognize his sin before the Lord.

2
The Law of Righteousness

Because of Adam's sin, men lived by their own standards. After destroying the world and scattering the people, God chose Abraham and his descendants. God delivered Abraham's descendants out of Egypt and gave them the law of righteousness.

At Mount Sinai, Moses and all of Israel gathered as God laid the foundation for righteousness. He instituted the Mosaic Law. The Law was a set of rules and regulations, instituted by God, which governed every aspect of man's life. At the heart of the Law were the Ten Commandments (Exodus 20:1-17).

The Law of Moses

From these commandments, we can identify the three main areas of man's existence that the Law addressed. The first was man's relationship with God (verses 1-3, 7). God instructed Israel to not serve any other gods, but Him. Their relationship with Him was to be exclusive. This was uncharacteristic of the time in which they lived. The majority of the countries worshiped more than one deity.

The second area addressed was man's worship of God (verses 4-6; 8-11). Israel was not to worship God in the same manner that the surrounding nations had in times past. They were not to make any images of God or creature, but keep the worship of God pure. The other nations forgot God through their idols and began to worship the creatures more than the Creator.

> ***And changed the glory of the uncorruptible God into an image made like to corruptible man, and to birds, and fourfooted beasts, and creeping things. Who changed the truth of God into a lie, and worshipped and served the creature more than the Creator, who is blessed forever. Amen. (Romans 1:23, 25)***

The Israelites were not to follow this pattern. In addition, they were instructed to set aside one day, in particular, to worship Him without distraction. They were not to call on His name using vain repetitions.

The third area addressed was man's relationship with one another (verses 12-17). They were instructed to treat one another with dignity and respect. They were to honor each other's families and property.

We learn, however, that Israel could not keep these commandments and they continually rebelled and sinned against God. The Bible teaches that the Law failed because it could not change the heart, nor purify the conscience of man.

> ***Seeing that that first [outer portion of the] tabernacle was a parable – a visible symbol or type or picture of the present age. In it gifts and sacrifices are offered, and yet are incapable of perfecting the conscience and renewing the inner man of the worshipper. (Hebrews 9:9 Amplified)***

The Law was not intended to offer them salvation, but lead them into the righteousness of God which is in Jesus. The Law, though it was good, could not make man righteous. It caused men to behold their sins.

> ***Wherefore the law is holy, and the commandment holy, and just, and good. Was then that which is good made death unto me? God forbid. But sin, that it might appear sin, working death in me by that which is good; that sin by***

> ***the commandment might become exceeding sinful. (Romans 7:12-13)***

Paul wrote to the Galatians and stated that if there was a law given that could bring men into righteousness, it was the Law. However, man proved that following principles and prerequisites could not bring men into inner righteousness.

> ***Is the law then against the promises of God? God forbid: for if there had been a law given which could have given life, verily righteousness should have been by the law. (Galatians 3:21)***

The 'Law' of the Pharisees

Because of the weakness of the Law, Israel failed to please God. In Jesus' day, the Pharisees substituted works for righteousness. They missed God's righteousness by establishing their own.

> ***For they being ignorant of God's righteousness, and going about to establish their own righteousness, have not submitted themselves unto the righteousness of God. (Romans 10:3)***

They wanted to appear righteous, without being righteous. During His earthly ministry, Jesus condemned the Pharisees on many occasions for failing to allow righteousness to come from their heart and not their works. It has always been the temptation of man to establish his own righteousness in place of God. This is what Eve did in the garden (discussed earlier). The Pharisees developed their own version of the Law and taught it as the commandment of God.

> ***But in vain they do worship me, teaching for doctrines the commandments of men. (Matthew 15:9)***

The Pharisees continually condemned Jesus for His righteousness because of their lack of internal righteousness.

> ***But go ye and learn what that meaneth, I will have mercy, and not sacrifice: for I am not come to call the righteous, but sinners to repentance. (Matthew 12:7)***

In addition, Jesus exhorted His listeners against being like them. He revealed that the righteousness of the servants of the Lord were to exceed that demonstrated by the Pharisees.

> ***For verily I say unto you, that except your righteousness shall exceed the righteousness of the scribes and Pharisees, ye shall in no case enter into the kingdom of heaven. (Matthew 5:20)***

How was this to be done? True followers of God will not only have righteous works, but righteous hearts also. That is, they will not only do what is right, but righteousness will be the driving force in their hearts and minds. The Law of righteousness, again, failed because:

1) **It did nothing for the conscience.** *Which was a figure for the time then present, in which were offered both gifts and sacrifices, that could not make him that did the service perfect, as pertaining to the conscience. (Hebrews 9:9)*

2) **It continually reminded man of his sin.** *Moreover the law entered, that the offence might abound. But where sin abounded, grace did much more abound. (Romans 5:20)*

3) **It was to bring us to the knowledge of Christ.** *Wherefore the law was our schoolmaster to bring us unto Christ, that we might be justified by faith. (Galatians 3:24)*

Though the Law condemned men, God provided a way for man to attain to His righteousness. Through Christ, man's righteousness would not come by works, but by God's gift.

3
The Gift of Righteousness

Under the New Covenant, man becomes righteous by God's gift. As believers, we believe unto righteousness. Just as Abraham believed God and it was counted unto him for righteousness. Abraham believed in the Lord that gave him a promise. He received the righteousness that is of God by faith, and not works.

> ***For what saith the scripture? Abraham believed God, and it was counted unto him for righteousness. (Romans 4: 3)***

Positional Righteousness

God counts us righteous on the inside before we do any work on the outside. Thus, God has imputed righteousness to us without works, but by faith. This is referred to as positional righteousness. Therefore, we have righteousness on the inside of us before exercising it. We obtain this gift of righteousness when we accept Jesus Christ.

> ***For with the heart man believeth unto righteousness; and with the mouth confession is made unto salvation. (Romans 10:10)***

When we believe on the Lord, God calls us His children and we are righteous. This is called positional righteousness. David experienced this in his life and ministry.

> ***Even as David also describeth the blessedness of the man, unto whom God imputeth righteousness without works. (Romans 4: 6)***

Even after David's sin, God did not judge him as a sinner. He continued to deal with David as His servant. Though David operated in sin, God did not count him as unrighteous. This serves as a model to believers. Though some may sin, it does not make them sinners. If they confess, repent, and continue in their walk with the Lord, they fulfill that which is written in Proverbs,

> ***For a just man falleth seven times, and riseth up again: but the wicked shall fall into mischief. (Proverbs 24:16)***

Positional righteousness protects us from God's judgment as we mature and grow in Him. This is the first dimension of the gift of righteousness. We are righteous because He says so, not because we always do that which is right. However, a sign of righteousness in the believer is confession and repentance.

> ***My little children, these things write I unto you, that ye sin not. And if any man sin, we have an advocate with the Father, Jesus Christ the righteous. (I John 2:1)***

Conditional Righteousness

Another dimension to the gift of righteousness is conditional righteousness. Conditional righteousness reflects the character and integrity that is resident within the believer. However, conditional righteousness is not something to be achieved by the believer's own strength and volition. We develop conditional righteousness by the fruit of the Spirit.

> ***But the fruit of the Spirit is love, joy, peace, longsuffering, gentleness, goodness, faith, meekness, temperance: against such there is no law. (Galatians 5: 22-23)***

As Adam and Eve ate of the fruit of the Tree of knowledge and became sinners, the believers can partake of the fruit of the Spirit and increase in righteousness. God gives this fruit to us to help us as we walk in godliness.

In the above verse, notice that faith is one of the fruit of the Spirit. These fruits are produced by the Spirit and not by man. Faith is required to obtain righteousness. Therefore, God produces faith in us in order for us to obtain righteousness. God produces faith in us by His Word.

> ***So then faith cometh by hearing, and hearing by the word of God. (Romans 10: 17)***

As we walk in the Spirit, we will not fulfill the desires of the flesh. Thus, we will develop righteousness in our daily lives. Again, conditional righteousness is achieved as we partake of the fruit of the Spirit.

Christ and the Gift of Righteousness

The gift of righteousness comes from Christ because of the work He did on earth. Christ fulfilled the Law and imputed His righteousness on us through the work He did on the cross.

> ***For if by one man's offence death reigned by one; much more they which receive abundance of grace and of the gift of***

righteousness shall reign in life by one, Jesus Christ. (Romans 5: 17)

But now the righteousness of God without the law is manifested, being witnessed by the law and the prophets; Even the righteousness of God which is by faith of Jesus Christ unto all and upon all them that believe: for there is no difference. (Romans 3: 21-22)

In this scripture, it states that now the righteousness of God without the Law is manifested. The righteousness of God is revealed in Jesus Christ. He is the fulfillment of the Law. He is the word made flesh. Believers are able to receive positional and conditional righteousness through Christ. Christ's coming brought an end to the Law and the beginning of the Law of liberty.

For Christ is the end of the law for righteousness to every one that believeth. (Romans 10:4)

Christ delivered us from the Law and the works that it demanded. The Law kept man in bondage. One had to live by the rules and requirements or be condemned.

For Moses describeth the righteousness which is of the law, That the man which

> ***doeth those things shall live by them. (Romans 10:5)***

The Law demanded obedience to outward works and rituals. If one failed to keep them, the Law judged him. However, because of the gift of righteousness through Christ, if one fails, he is not condemned but offered grace to help. This enables him to retain his righteousness. He remains righteous in spite of failure.

> ***There is therefore now no condemnation to them which are in Christ Jesus, who walk not after the flesh, but after the Spirit. (Romans 8:1)***

Again, righteousness is a gift. The only way to obtain it is by faith. After receiving righteousness, it is to be exercised. This is to be done through the aid of the Holy Spirit. In this, we should praise God daily for His provisions in righteousness.

4
The Gift of Righteousness & the Believer

In the previous section, we provided an answer to the question, "How do we obtain the righteousness of God?" We obtain the righteousness of God through Christ by faith.

> ***And be found in him, not having mine own righteousness, which is of the law, but that which is through the faith of Christ, the righteousness which is of God by faith: (Philippians 3: 9)***

Paul in verse 8 of Philippians chapter 3 stated that he counted all things but loss, for the excellency of the knowledge of Christ. In other words, the righteousness that he gained through the Judaic Law was nothing.

Paul forsook the righteousness that he gained through the Law for the righteousness that is in God through Christ by faith.

Deny Ourselves

In this section, we want to explore how the believer is to walk in true righteousness. We know that it is a gift and the Holy Spirit aids us in producing righteous characters. However, there is a part that we play.

The first step in walking in true righteousness is that we deny ourselves. We are to flee from unrighteous acts. The apostles repeatedly warned believers against immorality.

> ***Mortify therefore your members which are upon the earth; fornication, uncleanness, inordinate affection, evil concupiscence, and covetousness, which is idolatry: For which things' sake the wrath of God cometh on the children of disobedience. (Colossians 3:5-6)***

Paul instructed the Colossians to put to death wickedness, warning them that God's wrath would be the result. Though God counts us righteous, He expects us to have righteous acts. We are to crucify the works of the flesh.

> ***Now the works of the flesh are manifest, which are these; adultery, fornication, uncleanness, lasciviousness, idolatry, witchcraft, hatred, variance, emulations,***

> ***wrath, strife, seditions, heresies, envyings, murders, drunkenness, revellings, and such like: of the which I tell you before, as I have also told you in time past, that they which do such things shall not inherit the kingdom of God. (Galatians 5:19-21)***

If we are going to walk in righteousness, then the works, desires, and lusts of the flesh have to be put to death. All forms of sexual immorality (fornication, adultery, homosexuality, and the like), all forms of uncleanness, drunkenness, lying, and all unrighteousness have to be forsaken.

Deny Opinions and False Doctrines

Other religions and sects require self-denial in order to obtain right standing with God, but without Christ, they are still operating in self-righteousness.

Self-righteousness (discussed earlier) is in operation when men exalt their own opinions and ideas above God. They worship their own opinions and thoughts over God. God's thoughts and ways are above our thoughts and ways.

> ***For as the heavens are higher than the earth, so are my ways higher than your ways, and my thoughts than your thoughts. (Isaiah 55:9)***

When we worship something or someone, we submit to or follow it. If we worship God, then we must submit ourselves to Him completely. Jesus told the Samaritan woman at the well that those that worship God must worship Him in spirit and in truth.

> ***Ye worship ye know not what: we know what we worship: for salvation is of the Jews. But the hour cometh, and now is, when the true worshippers shall worship the Father in spirit and in truth: for the Father seeketh such to worship him. God is a Spirit: and they that worship him must worship him in spirit and in truth. (John 4:22-24)***

In this verse, the word *spirit* means sincerity. Jesus was telling the woman that the only way to worship God is to mean it completely and with the right information. In this verse, the word *truth* means the right information.

Throughout biblical history man has strayed away from what God has set up. God gave Moses the Law, but man have strayed away from what the Law was originally designed to do. It was designed to bring man back into relationship with God.

The righteousness that was in the Law, Israel had missed. Consider the following scripture,

> ***But Israel, which followed after the law of righteousness, hath not attained to the law of righteousness. (Romans 9:31)***

Some believers today have made gods out of their opinions and doctrines. Like the Pharisees, some have established their own righteousness. They forget they are righteous by faith.

Our character plays a greater part in our righteousness with God than our teachings and ministry. Sometimes we teach the wrong information or misuse scriptures that may cause us to operate in self-righteousness. This will lead to ungodliness.

> ***But shun profane and vain babblings: for they will increase unto more ungodliness. (2 Timothy 2:16)***

Some doctrines we need to put away in order to see clearly God's standards. Paul warned Timothy against vain sayings and teachings because they produced unrighteousness in believers.

Therefore, in order to walk in righteousness, the believer has to forsake sin. In addition, he is to forsake doctrines and opinions that will lead them into ungodliness. In doing so, the believer will be able to receive the rewards of righteousness.

5
The Reward of Righteousness

In the previous sections, we have discussed the beginning of righteousness, the law of righteousness, the gift of righteousness, and walking in righteousness. Though righteousness makes demands of the believer, it is not without reason. There is a reward for those who receive and walk in God's gift of righteousness. The gift of righteousness has a two-fold reward. Consider Jesus' words.

> ***And every one that hath forsaken houses, or brethren, or sisters, or father, or mother, or wife, or children, or lands, for my name's sake, shall receive an hundredfold, and shall inherit everlasting life. (Matthew 19:29)***

Two-fold Reward of Righteousness

Jesus revealed that those who followed Him in righteousness would have reward in this life and in the life to come. Herein is the two-fold reward of righteousness. If we walk in righteousness, we will experience God's provision and comfort now and forever.

> ***For the kingdom of God is not meat and drink; but righteousness, and peace, and joy in the Holy Ghost. (Romans 14:17)***

If we walk in righteousness, we can expect God's provision, protection, and power in this life. Righteousness brings us into the favor of God and the respect of men. As Jesus grew, because He pleased God, He experienced this. We will have the same testimony if we walk in His gift of righteousness.

> ***And Jesus increased in wisdom and stature, and in favour with God and man. (Luke 2:52)***

Aside from favor with God and man in this life, we will receive the reward of eternal life.

> ***That as sin hath reigned unto death, even so might grace reign through righteousness unto eternal life by Jesus Christ our Lord. (Romans 5:21)***

From this verse, we discover that righteousness leads us to eternal life through Christ. We do not forsake sin and ungodliness for nothing. We will be rewarded, if we stand in faith.

> ***Henceforth there is laid up for me a crown of righteousness, which the Lord, the righteous judge, shall give me at that day: and not to me only, but unto all them also that love his appearing. (2 Timothy 4:8)***

We can expect to receive eternal life and rewards for our labors and service unto the Lord. Righteousness and godliness has reward in this life and in the one that is to come.

> ***For bodily exercise profiteth little: but godliness is profitable unto all things, having promise of the life that now is, and of that which is to come. (I Timothy 4:8)***

The Fulfillment of Righteousness

The scriptures repeatedly assert that the fulfillment of the Law and the commandments of God rest in love.

> ***Jesus said unto him, Thou shalt love the Lord thy God with all thy heart, and with all thy soul, and with all thy mind. This is the first and great commandment. And the second is like unto it, Thou shalt love thy neighbour as thyself. On these two***

> ***commandments hang all the law and the prophets. (Matthew 22:37-40)***

Walking in love is the ultimate fulfillment of righteousness. We demonstrate that we are sons and daughters as we walk in love.

> ***But love ye your enemies, and do good, and lend, hoping for nothing again; and your reward shall be great, and ye shall be the children of the Highest: for he is kind unto the unthankful and to the evil. (Luke 6:35)***

Love is powerful. It causes us to walk in righteousness. If we love, we will want to do that which is right. Moreover, we will actually do that which is right.

Let us remember Paul's words concerning love. If we say the love of God is in us, we will demonstrate the words in this familiar passage. Love causes us to act righteously and with the right motives.

> ***Though I speak with the tongues of men and of angels, and have not charity, I am become as sounding brass, or a tinkling cymbal. And though I have the gift of prophecy, and understand all mysteries, and all knowledge; and though I have all faith, so that I could remove mountains,***

> ***and have not charity, I am nothing. And though I bestow all my goods to feed the poor, and though I give my body to be burned, and have not charity, it profiteth me nothing. Charity suffereth long, and is kind; charity envieth not; charity vaunteth not itself, is not puffed up, Doth not behave itself unseemly, seeketh not her own, is not easily provoked, thinketh no evil; Rejoiceth not in iniquity, but rejoiceth in the truth; beareth all things, believeth all things, hopeth all things, endureth all things. (I Corinthians 13:1-7)***

Love causes us to put righteousness into action from the heart. It will not be vain or with partiality. James says that if we love (and have faith), we will show it in our good works.

> ***What doth it profit, my brethren, though a man say he hath faith, and have not works? can faith save him? If a brother or sister be naked, and destitute of daily food, And one of you say unto them, Depart in peace, be ye warmed and filled; notwithstanding ye give them not those things which are needful to the body; what doth it profit? (James 2:14-16)***

Faith combined with love completes righteousness in the believer. God is love. If we believe this, then it will be expressed in our daily activities. When we walk in faith and love, which produces righteousness, we will receive our eternal reward, which is life with Christ forever. If we walk in love, our reward in heaven is secured.

Other Books and Series from Christopher C. Young

The Gift of Righteousness - ***Exploring Issues in Righteousness*:** What is righteousness? How can I know that I am right with God? These questions have been the subject of controversy since the Church's early existence. However, the Christian has to understand that righteousness is in who we are and not what we do. More importantly, the Christian has to realize that ultimately righteousness is a gift. In this book, we will explore issues in righteousness while giving believers an appreciation for God's gift of righteousness.

Manna for Prayer - ***Lessons in Prayer from Abraham*:** One of the important features of the Christian Life is prayer. Without prayer, no Christian would be victorious in attempting to live godly in Christ. Therefore, a clear and complete understanding of prayer is vital. In this publication, we will receive some valuable manna for prayer from Abraham. He was a man of faith and prayer. From the story of his search for a wife for his son, Isaac, we will discover some valuable truth concerning prayer. These some truths will benefit the believer today.

If you would like to purchase these publications, please visit us on-line at www.lulu.com/freshmanna

www.ingramcontent.com/pod-product-compliance
Lightning Source LLC
LaVergne TN
LVHW052302100826
845147LV00001B/117